Old KIRKINTILLOCH
by
Guthrie Hutton

Kiln Close, which ran off the High Street at Kirkintilloch Cross, was where Burns' Bakery operated. It is seen here in the 1920s, the antithesis of the polished hygiene of today's food factories, and yet Burns', and other small bakeries like it, added something to a community. They cooked up variety and taste, but above all they produced that delicious morning smell of new baked bread which awoke the senses and made folk feel glad to be alive.

© Guthrie Hutton 2004
First published in the United Kingdom, 2004,
by Stenlake Publishing Ltd.
01290 551122
www.stenlake.co.uk

ISBN 9781840333008

Ptinted by P2D Books, 1 Newlands Rd,
Westoning, Bedford, MK45 5LD

The publishers regret that they cannot supply copies of any pictures featured in this book.

ACKNOWLEDGEMENTS

I am deeply indebted to Don Martin of East Dunbartonshire Libraries, the William Patrick Library, Kirkintilloch, for his considerable help with this publication. Many of the pictures come from the magnificent photographic archive he and his colleagues have built up over many years, and having access to this resource has enhanced this book considerably. I am also grateful to Don and his colleagues for their assistance in digging out research material and their politeness when dealing with daft questions. Their unfailing good humour marks Kirkintilloch out as one of the pleasanter places to research local history. I am also grateful to Miss Fletcher who let me use the pictures on pages 14 and 16 and shared some interesting memories with me.

FURTHER READING

Strathkelvin District Libraries and Museums (now East Dunbartonshire Libraries and Museums), have published a number of very fine local history books. Those consulted in the preparation of this publication include:

Bowman, A. I., *Kirkintilloch Shipbuilding*, 1983
Bowman, A. I., *Swifts & Queens*, 1984
Bowman, A. I., *The Gipsy o' Kirky*, 1987
Carter, Paul (ed.), *Forth & Clyde Canal Guidebook*, 1985 (revised 1991 & 2001)
Martin, Don, *The Forth & Clyde Canal, a Kirkintilloch View*, 1977
Martin, Don, *The Story of Kirkintilloch*, 1980
Martin, Don, and MacLean, A. A., *Edinburgh & Glasgow Railway Guidebook*, 1992
Martin, Don, and Selwyn, Sue, *Kirkintilloch Life & Times*, 1994

By other publishers:

Keppie, Lawrence, *Scotland's Roman Remains*, 1986 (revised 1990)
Martin, Don, *Kirkintilloch in Old Picture Postcards*, 1985
Saltire Society, *Scotland's Most Alive Small Burgh*, 1961
Watson, Thomas, *Kirkintilloch: Town and Parish*, 1894

On 1 January 2000, while most of the population was nursing a giant collective hangover, Don Martin of the William Patrick Library was out with his camera. Don knew that the first day of the new millennium had great significance and that in years to come a photographic record, taken on that day, would gain in historical value and be a great asset for the future custodians of Kirkintilloch's history. He captured an interesting detail at the Townhead canal bridge where the signs and road layout contradict each other. This was because the contractor had to open the road for the festive season, so Don's picture is a rare record of a scene which existed for only a few days. This is the very essence of local history; it happens around us every day and, unlike great events which pass us by, it touches everyone. The trick is to be aware, to notice and be excited, because this story is real, and we are all part of it.

INTRODUCTION

Kirkintilloch's place in history was assured when the Romans built a fort on the ridge south-west of the confluence of the River Kelvin and Luggie Water. It was set behind the empire's most northerly frontier, the Antonine Wall, a great turf and timber rampart thrown up about AD 143 between the Forth and Clyde estuaries. A millennium or so later, a castle was built close to where the Romans had erected their fort and the town that grew up around it continued to thrive or struggle through good times and bad until the latter part of the eighteenth century. That was when the next great structure to cross Scotland, the Forth & Clyde Canal, was driven past the southern edge of the town.

The canal became more to Kirkintilloch than just a transport route. It brought industry and a pioneering railway, and local people identified with it in a way that did not happen elsewhere. They built and operated boats for both cargo and passengers, and if the canal made modern Kirkintilloch then the favour was reciprocated. When the waterway reopened in 2001, after nearly 40 years of closure, local politicians called Kirkintilloch 'The Canal Capital of Scotland', and they were right.

The heavy industry brought by the canal gradually took over from the occupation that had formerly been the townspeople's principal activity: weaving. Weavers worked alone, only gathering together when they had time to talk, and when that talk turned to politics it was usually radical in nature. The added influence of iron-workers, canalmen, railwaymen and miners saw Kirkintilloch's tradition of radical politics take root. It spawned one of Scotland's most prominent politicians of the twentieth century, Tom Johnston, who rose from being a town councillor to become Secretary of State for Scotland between 1941 and 1945 in the wartime coalition government. The council buildings at Whitegates were named Tom Johnston House in his honour.

Local government in Kirkintilloch began to change in 1836 when it was elevated to the status of a police burgh. This was overseen by police commissioners, but local people were unhappy with the partly-appointed, partly-elected status of these officials and took advantage of the General Police and Improvement Act of 1862 to have the burgh area redefined and new commissioners elected. They began work in 1871 and, because they were in effect a town council, this title was adopted in 1901. The council initiated a variety of pioneering services including the country's first municipal bank and a herd of municipal goats: of these, the bank was a success! They also tackled housing problems with such vigour that the burgh boundaries had to be pushed outwards to absorb the expansion. Some of that housing was also tied to the establishment of new light industry as part of Glasgow overspill schemes.

In 1975 the town council was replaced by Strathkelvin District Council and twenty years later this was superseded by East Dunbartonshire Council. Kirkintilloch has continued to change with the times and, at the start of another millennium, is again poised to build on the foundations of the past to ensure its future.

Looking north along Cowgate towards High Street with the Barony Chambers and steeple on the left.

The Romans' fort was in the vicinity of Peel Park overlooking the Campsie Hills and the Kelvin Valley, and the castle that followed in medieval times stood in the same general location. It was probably built in the twelfth century and would have initially been an earthen bank topped with a timber fortification. This had almost certainly become more sophisticated by the early 1300s when it was garrisoned by English soldiers and attracted the hostile interest of King Robert the Bruce's supporters. After his victory at Bannockburn, Bruce set about destroying the castles that had held out against him, and it may well be that Kirkintilloch's was one of these. Whatever its fate, it had ceased to exist long before the late nineteenth century when all that remained was the earthen bank, which – along with the surrounding land – was being used as a dairy farm. It was known as the Peel, a word derived from the original wooden palisade surrounding the castle. The town council, or police commissioners as they were at that time, acquired the land in 1897 and opened it as a public park the following year. It was intended to commemorate Queen Victoria's Diamond Jubilee, so they called it Victoria Park, but local people continued to call it the Peel and that's the name that has stuck.

Peel Park was initially envisaged as a pleasant open space where people could enjoy some peace, away from the hubbub of the town. It had no facilities, however, and it seems that Kirky folk were unimpressed until a fountain and a bandstand were installed in 1905. They were donated by prominent citizens: the bandstand by Bailie Perry (who later became provost of the burgh) and the fountain by ex-Bailie Hudson, managing director of the Lion Foundry. The two cast-iron structures were made at the Lion Foundry and proved to be popular with local people, particularly the bandstand which served as a useful platform for visiting and local bands alike. Kirkintilloch has a fine tradition of band music, with the Kirkintilloch Silver Band carrying on from the Rechabite Band, one of the regulars in the early days of the park bandstand. On the right of this picture of the park's new facilities is the Holy Family and St Ninian Church in Union Street. It was erected in 1893 to take the place of a smaller hall which had served as a place of worship for the Catholic population since 1875. The hall had also doubled as a school, and in 1895 a new school was built on an adjacent site fronting on to Union Street.

High Street runs across the northern edge of Kirkintilloch, rising steeply from east and west. The hills were hard work for cart horses (holding a cart going downhill was every bit as strenuous as hauling it up), and for those not actually going into the town it was a lot of pain for no gain. The equine dream of a level road came true c.1805 when a very early town bypass was made to the north of the old High Street. The new road can be seen on the left of this view, which also shows West High Street heading up the hill on the right. The bypass was one of a number of new roads built at the time to improve transport links around the country, but these projects were not publicly funded and were instead financed by private trustees who were allowed to charge tolls to recoup their costs. A toll-house still stands (just out of sight to the left in this picture) with a recreated table of tolls on the wall. Gates known as turnpikes were used to stop the traffic while the tolls were collected, a contrast to the present-day roundabout which is designed to keep the traffic moving through what is now a very busy junction.

Opposite: This picture of East High Street, foreshortened by a zoom lens, gives an excellent impression of the way the town rises up to the Barony Chambers. If one conjures up an image of an imposing castle instead of the distinctive steeple, the medieval burgh that might have been is readily brought to mind. Such a trick is harder to perform today because the new bypass road has cut through the line of the old High Street and altered the shape of the town. The town cross used to stand at the crest of the High Street hills but was destroyed in an act of vandalism in 1815. Angered townspeople placed the pieces of broken stone in the Luggie Water for safekeeping, but they became silted over and lost. At the base of the hill, East High Street crosses the swift-flowing Luggie Water and, because a ford was never a practical option on such a busy road, a bridge has existed here for many years. The iron and stone structure in this picture was rebuilt in the 1880s to replace an all-stone one from the late eighteenth century. In the foreground is the monument erected to commemorate Hazelton Robert Robson, a seventeen year old Glasgow boy who drowned while trying to rescue a child from the flooded river in 1876. Following severe floods in December 1994, a heavy, concrete flood defence wall was erected between the monument and the river. It forms part of an extensive system of flood defences that have changed the look of the northern side of town.

THOMPSON'S
WAREHOUSE
FOR CHINA GLASS

This view again emphasises the medieval origins of the town. It looks west from the railway bridge over Eastside and leads the eye towards the Luggie Bridge and up East High Street to the Barony Chambers. These were erected in 1815 on the site of the old tolbooth, and like their predecessor were the focus of civic affairs in the town, being used at times as a courthouse, jail, town hall and school. In the early twentieth century, before the rise of the Labour Party, East High Street and Eastside could be regarded as the centre of local politics. The Conservative Hall was erected in East High Street in 1906, and in this picture its domed turret can be seen to the right of the Barony Chambers' steeple. The distinctive tenement in the right foreground was where the Liberal Party met, and is known as both Belmont Terrace and the Liberal Buildings. It was erected in 1900, replacing the cottages with corbie-stepped gables and thatched roofs on the left of the picture on the facing page. Viewed from the distance of time, such buildings had character and charm, but they no doubt suffered from the problems that afflicted many of Scotland's old town buildings: damp, neglect and an absence of sanitation. A lack of the means – or will – to effect improvements meant that much of the country's vernacular town architecture, including that in Kirkintilloch, disappeared during the first half of the twentieth century.

The old cottages of Eastside are certainly damp in this picture of a flood from 1897. As well as showing how vulnerable Eastside was to the Luggie's periodic overflows, it also illustrates that it was a very wide street, and it was this feature that made it possible to hold a weekly lint or linen market here. Spinning and weaving linen were important occupations in Kirkintilloch, and so the Eastside market would have had great importance as a place where people could buy and sell products at various stages in the linen-making process. Linen-weaving was largely superseded by cotton in the nineteenth century, and so the lint market had ceased long before this picture was taken. Some of the old Eastside cottages, however, survived into the twentieth century, although little if anything had been done to improve them. One was owned by potato merchant W. & A. Graham who used it as a bothy to house casual farm-workers, such as the Irish potato pickers from Achill Island, County Mayo, who were staying there in September 1937. They were asleep when a fire broke out during the night. Ten men were trapped and died, while the foreman and a boy got out and the women in the neighbouring room escaped through a broken window. The tragedy highlighted the plight of people who had to labour for long hours and live in communal squalor to provide cheap food for others.

The Liberal Buildings and the Barony Chambers' steeple are amongst the landmarks in the background of this view looking across the Forth & Clyde Canal at Hillhead Bridge. The canal played a large part in the development of Kirkintilloch. Work to cut it began at Grangemouth in June 1768 and it had reached Hillhead Basin by 1773: the basin was also known as Port Hillhead, or Kirkintilloch Harbour. In a bid to earn some money, the cash-strapped canal company put this completed section in water and with Hillhead Basin as its western terminal began trading operations. Goods destined for Glasgow were unloaded at the basin and taken by cart to the city, while the same process operated in reverse for cargoes going east. This trade made Hillhead Scotland's first true inland port. The wood and iron bascule bridge spanning the canal here was replaced in 1938 with a steel swing bridge which was put back into use when the canal reopened in 2001. It was necessary to have an opening bridge because Hillhead is so high above the surrounding area that an impossibly steep access road would have been required to get over a fixed bridge at the new standard headroom of three metres above the water.

Over time, the small community on the east side of Hillhead Bridge acquired a reputation for drunkenness, poverty and lawlessness. When the men worked, it was mainly on the canal or in the mines, and when there was trouble – as during a canal boatmen's strike in 1904 – the womenfolk took to defending their community by throwing stones at 'blackleg' crews taking boats through the bridge. Hillhead women and children were also adept at obtaining their winter fuel from the coal boats that tied up in the canal basin. They usually managed to raid the unsecured cargoes and make a coal-blackened getaway before the local constabulary could react. This 1959 picture of a cold-looking Hillhead Road makes it easy to understand why people would want to pinch coal to keep warm. The houses seen here were demolished shortly after the picture was taken and the area redeveloped, with housing eventually spreading along the south bank of the canal to Harestanes. The buildings illustrated were typical of the area, and some had earth floors up to the 1950s. Hillhead Road was the location of the last thatched house in Kirkintilloch.

Hillhead's prominence diminished as the canal was opened up to Stockingfield (Maryhill) by 1775, Hamilton Hill (Glasgow) by 1777, and – after overcoming financial difficulties – to Bowling in 1790. Although the centre of action had moved further west, Hillhead Basin remained important as the base for a number of boats, so many in fact that when they were all in port on a Sunday people could walk from one side of the basin to the other across them. Many boatmen lived at Hillhead and timed their journeys so that they could stop there for a break. This could mean anything from nipping home for a hurried meal or a few hours' sleep, to savouring a drink at the Waterloo Inn, a canalside hostelry that advertised a range of beverages and a commitment to attend to family orders punctually! Boats usually travelled with open hatches and it wasn't just local people who raided the cargoes of coal – other boatmen simply tied up alongside and helped themselves to fuel for their bunkers or stoves. An open-hatched lighter is seen here on the right, while the pleasure steamer *Gipsy Queen* passes through Hillhead Basin on her way back to Glasgow. She was one of three Kirkintilloch-owned steamers, the others being *Fairy Queen* and *May Queen*.

Gipsy Queen can be seen here on the aqueduct over the Luggie Water. The river presented the canal engineers with a formidable obstacle and they tackled it with élan, creating a structure without equal in 1770s Scotland, although to some extent the need to build such a large aqueduct was self-imposed. Engineer John Smeaton originally planned to cross the river further upstream, but his assistant on the ground, Robert Mackell, persuaded him to bring the canal closer to the town. Mackell also appears to have modified some details of Smeaton's plans for the aqueduct itself. The span of the arch was 50 feet and it was 90 feet deep to accommodate the full breadth of the canal. To build such a large structure economically the contractors, who hailed from Falkirk, made the aqueduct in three sections, moving the wooden former – or centring – after each section was completed. The work was done so well that the joins are very hard to detect. The span of the arch was so generous that engineers laying the Campsie Branch Railway (see page 34) in the 1840s were able to take its tracks under the aqueduct on a masonry platform sandwiched between the canal and the river. Kirkintilloch folk called this canal/railway combination the 'Unique Bridge', and so it was!

Townhead Bridge carried the main north/south road through the town over the Forth & Clyde Canal. At this point the canal also had to cut through high ground, and the bridge is at a higher level than the one at Hillhead. This type of bridge, a counterbalanced bascule, was adopted as standard after 1790. It replaced the original bridges which were like those on Dutch canals with overhead ballast beams acting as counterweights. With increasing volumes of road traffic, the bascule bridge was replaced by a steel swing bridge in 1933 and, when the canal closed in the 1960s, a drowned culvert was installed. This allowed water to flow through submerged pipes, but blocked the surface and caused a build-up of stinking, rotting weed and rubbish on either side. The mess was consigned to history in May 2000 when the bridge was reopened for canal boats, and exactly a year later a parade of vessels passed through to celebrate the reopening of the whole canal from coast to coast. This view shows the pre-1933 bridge with some of the Hay family's cargo boats beyond. Such vessels were known as scows or lighters: the distinction is hard to pin down, but in the late nineteenth and early twentieth centuries the *Kirkintilloch Herald* consistently referred to horse-hauled barges as scows, and the larger, steam-powered vessels as lighters. Some lighters also operated outside the canal, on the Clyde, where they became known as 'puffers' and were immortalised, along with their crews, in the stories of Para Handy and the *Vital Spark*.

John Hay operated both scows and lighters and kept his boats in good order at a repair slipway off Southbank Road. This only provided sporadic work, and to keep the men employed he started to build boats at what appears to modern eyes to be an impossibly constricted site beside Townhead Bridge, at the foot of the steep bank below Southbank Road. The yard launched its first boat at the end of the 1860s and its last, the *Chindit*, in 1945, while the company of J. & J. Hay was still operating lighters up to and beyond the canal's closure. As well as this cargo-carrying activity, Kirkintilloch also had a close association with the canal's passenger craft. Alexander Taylor, the owner of the Eagle Inn, the building in the centre of this picture, took over the running of the fast horse-drawn service between Glasgow and Falkirk from the canal company in the 1840s and sought to improve it in 1860 with a steamer, *Rockvilla Castle*. She was taken over in 1875 by another Kirkintilloch man, George Aitken, and it was his son James who started the canal pleasure steamer operation in 1893. His first boat was *Fairy Queen*, which he replaced in 1897 with a second vessel of the same name. He added the *May Queen*, seen here in front of the Eagle Inn, in 1903. She was built by another Kirkintilloch boat builder, Peter McGregor & Co., at the company's yard in the railway basin.

The Union Canal was opened in 1822, running from Edinburgh to a junction with the Forth & Clyde Canal at Falkirk. Although it didn't come near Kirkintilloch, the new canal had a big impact on the town – or maybe the impact was the other way round. It was made to get coal into Edinburgh from the west, but the big western coalfield was the Monklands and the only way to transport the coal to Edinburgh was to first move it into Glasgow along the Monkland Canal, and then back out on the Forth & Clyde. This cost time and money, and so the coalmasters decided to cut out the loop by building the Monkland & Kirkintilloch Railway, which was completed in 1826. Its route ran from the Coatbridge area to a jetty off Southbank Road, but this was quickly superseded by the trans-shipment basin seen here. This view looking across the canal from Northbank Avenue also shows a steam lighter on Hay's repair slipway, behind the trees on the left. The basin was used to move coal to places other than Edinburgh, most notably Grangemouth docks. This trade led to an important innovation – a barge with rails on the deck allowing loaded coal carts to be run aboard – a technique that saved large lumps of coal from being broken up by double handling, an important consideration at a time when 'big coal' commanded high prices and small pieces of coal and dross were hard to sell.

The Monkland & Kirkintilloch was a pioneering venture and put the town at the forefront of the development of two forms of transport: canals and railways. It was only the second public railway in Scotland, and the first to be laid with rails that could properly support steam locomotives. Although the railway's primary purpose was to move goods through – and not to – the town, it nevertheless acted as a spur for local businesses. Its canalside terminal meant that it was in the right place to service new industries like the nickel works to the west and the foundries to the east and west when they were set up on the south bank of the canal. The railway ran into Kirkintilloch along the line of the Bothlin Burn and crossed Lenzie Road where Tom Johnston House now stands. The road crossing was protected by white-painted level crossing gates which are the source of the local name, Whitegates. They also helped to define the boundary between Kirkintilloch and Lenzie. Road users, irritated by the occasional train using the level crossing, would no doubt have celebrated in 1966 when the railway closed, although the hold-ups at the present-day traffic lights can be just as irksome.

It was a dirty old world in those days of coal dust, soot and smoke, and the only alternative to washing things by hand was to send them to the laundry. A number of such businesses were set up in the Kirkintilloch area and one of these was the Vindanda Laundry. It appears to have been started in Lenzie about 1900 or 1901 by the Misses Davidson and Moir. Their reputation for care grew, and they soon had to expand to meet the needs of their growing list of customers. In 1910 they took over the works of the Kirkintilloch & Lenzie Steam Laundry Co. which had opened a new laundry at Whitegates in July 1906. The Misses Davidson and Moir made a point of maintaining prices and doing their work with the same care and dispatch as before. Vans collected and delivered laundry over a wide area and made frequent runs into Glasgow. The laundry regularly updated its equipment, and as part of this process a new landmark was added to the Whitegates area when a 65-foot chimney was erected in the early 1950s; it would stand for just over twenty years. Faced with competition from washing machines and laundrettes, the laundry closed in February 1971 and the chimney was demolished in November of that year.

An unremarkable collection of houses, cottages and weaving shops, Donaldson Street became the location of Townhead School in 1890. Education appears to have been something that Kirkintilloch folk took seriously, because prior to the Education Act of 1872 there were a number of parish and private schools offering at least some schooling to about half of the burgh's children. To modern perceptions this seems a very low figure, but in the mid-nineteenth century many places had much worse records, a situation that the 1872 Act sought to address by making schooling compulsory. Local authorities were required to provide schools, and parents had to ensure that their children attended. In Kirkintilloch, new schools were built at Lairdsland (1875) and Townhead. Over the years others were constructed to meet the needs of an expanding and changing population, with a large increase in this programme from the late 1950s to the early 1970s when many more children had to be catered for and some of the old schools had reached the end of their useful lives. Townhead School closed in 1981, exactly 50 years after these children posed for the camera.

This early twentieth century view of Townhead from Industry Street shows a very different road junction from the one that exists today. Then Industry Street was the main road to and from Cumbernauld, with traffic passing between the tenement on the right and the park and fountain in the foreground. The latter was erected in 1905, the same year that the fountain and bandstand in Peel Park were installed in what the *Kirkintilloch Herald* described as an 'epidemic of generosity'. The Industry Street fountain was donated by James D. G. Dalrymple, senior magistrate of the Burgh and Barony of Kirkintilloch, in memory of his uncle, James Dalrymple, who had been senior magistrate for 57 years. The office was something of a family tradition for the Dalrymples of Woodhead, going back to 1659 when the first of five family members was appointed. Woodhead House, which gave its name to Woodhead Park, was just behind Townhead, as was the Miners' Welfare Institute built in the mid-1920s. It sits at the back of the buildings on the left which have now been replaced by a modern block of flats and offices, one of which is used by the *Kirkintilloch Herald*. This has always been one of the best local papers and its reports on burgh life since 1884 make it a rich source of material for local historians. Indeed, the saying that 'journalism is the first draft of history' could well have been coined about it rather than the *Washington Post*.

The very name Industry Street seems to come from a bygone age when people applauded and encouraged industrial endeavour instead of wondering what had happened to it all. Not that Industry Street had much in the way of actual industry other than some weaving shops and a bridge over the Campsie Branch Railway. It ran from the junction at Townhead, seen on the facing page, to the burgh boundary just west of Holmfield, and for most of that length was lined with the kind of domestic architecture seen in this view looking west from the large house known as Myrtle Bank (out of sight behind the railings on the right). Windsor Crescent, the prominent tenement block seen on the right on the facing page, is visible in the centre background. It was built in stages between 1902 and 1904. Over the years Industry Street has suffered a number of changes to its line and length. In 1954 the section from Loch Road to the burgh boundary was renamed Waterside Road, and more recently it was cut in two by the creation of Parliament Road, which forms the link to Townhead Roundabout at the head of the town's bypass road. Most of the buildings on the right were situated where the new link road is now.

The links to the new bypass road have had a big impact on Townhead too. In this picture from the 1920s the junction of Lenzie Road is on the left. At that time traffic from Lenzie had to turn either left for the town centre, or right for Cumbernauld; now it can go straight on to the bypass following a line which has taken out the buildings to the right of William Dick's van. Beside Dick's butcher's shop was Connor's Grocery, which offered high-class provisions at keen prices. The owner, one of Townhead's most prominent traders, joined a 1923 campaign to persuade people to shop locally. 'Don't burden yourself with parcels from Glasgow, PURCHASE LOCALLY, and get the merchants to do the carrying for you', was the advice given in a positively worded advertisement in the *Kirky Herald*. Traders throughout the town today would welcome a few more folk heeding that! Another prominent Townhead trader was the Kirkintilloch Equitable Co-operative Society whose three-storey building, dating from 1913, can be seen in the centre background. The small two-storey building to its right was later rebuilt by the Co-op and used as a creamery. Other Co-op stores in Townhead sold clothing, footwear, groceries, fish, bread, meat and furniture. Another branch in Windsor Crescent at the corner of Industry Street dealt in radios, gramophones, bicycles and prams.

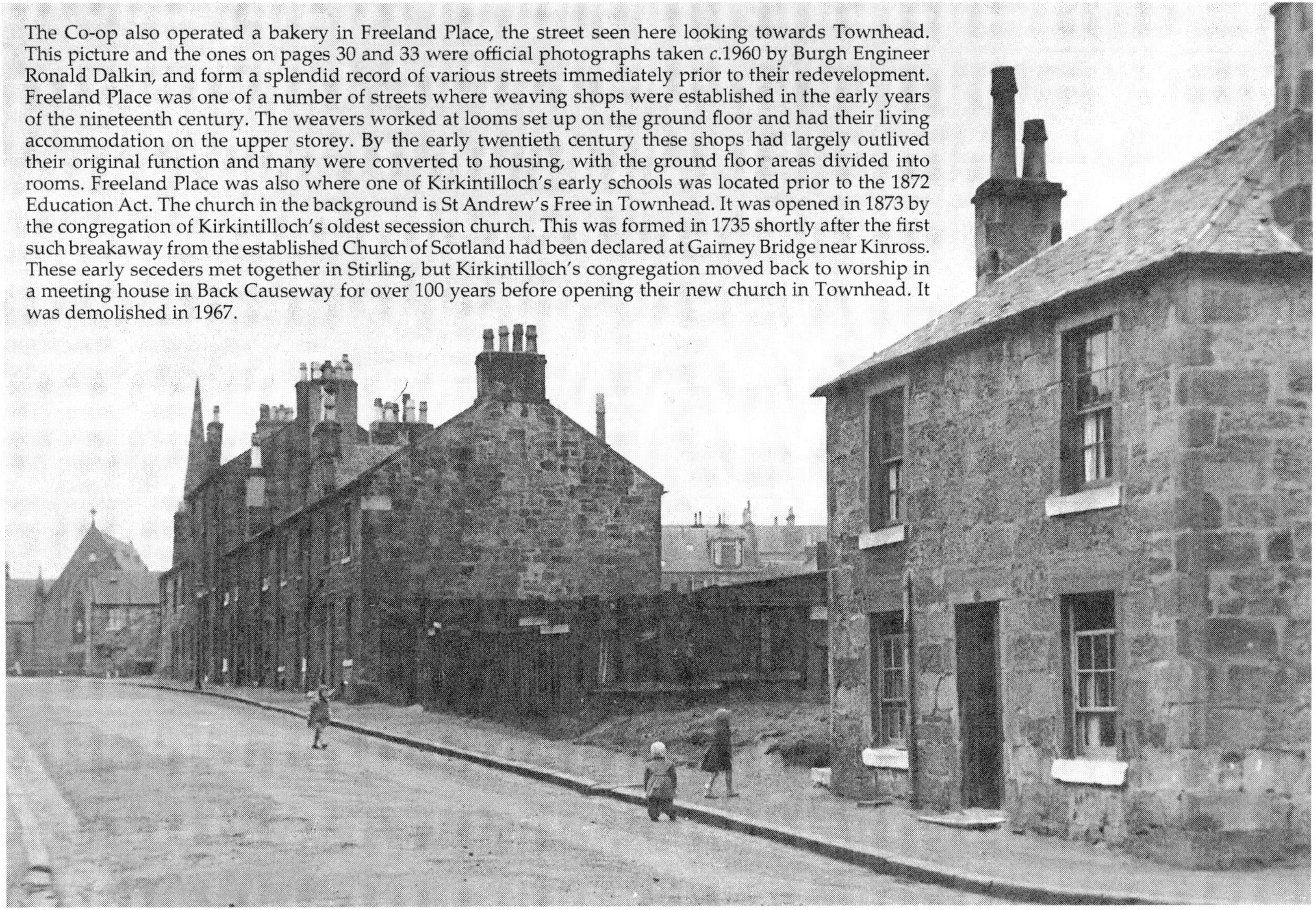

The Co-op also operated a bakery in Freeland Place, the street seen here looking towards Townhead. This picture and the ones on pages 30 and 33 were official photographs taken c.1960 by Burgh Engineer Ronald Dalkin, and form a splendid record of various streets immediately prior to their redevelopment. Freeland Place was one of a number of streets where weaving shops were established in the early years of the nineteenth century. The weavers worked at looms set up on the ground floor and had their living accommodation on the upper storey. By the early twentieth century these shops had largely outlived their original function and many were converted to housing, with the ground floor areas divided into rooms. Freeland Place was also where one of Kirkintilloch's early schools was located prior to the 1872 Education Act. The church in the background is St Andrew's Free in Townhead. It was opened in 1873 by the congregation of Kirkintilloch's oldest secession church. This was formed in 1735 shortly after the first such breakaway from the established Church of Scotland had been declared at Gairney Bridge near Kinross. These early seceders met together in Stirling, but Kirkintilloch's congregation moved back to worship in a meeting house in Back Causeway for over 100 years before opening their new church in Townhead. It was demolished in 1967.

The Co-op's first stores on Townhead were located at either end of the large tenement building on the right of this view looking south across the canal bridge. The building on the left, opposite the Co-op, was occupied on the ground floor by a pub called the Boar's Head. The bridge seems unusually quiet in this picture, even though it was taken before the First World War. Normally horse-drawn traffic was heavy and the little ridges in the centre of bridge were there to give the horses a better grip on the slippery wooden surface. The fenced footpath section beside the roadway was also uncommon and a clear indication that this bridge was on a busy road. With the growth in road transport after the First World War the bridge became a legendary traffic bottleneck. Its hold-ups were so famous that even national newspapers carried stories about them as a campaign for a new bridge gathered pace. It ultimately bore fruit and work to replace the 'Auld Brig' began in October 1932. The road was dug up again in the 1960s when the bridge was replaced by a culvert, and more disruption attended the building of a new fixed bridge for the reopened canal in 2000/2001. Kirkintilloch's road users will be hoping the planners have got it right this time!

Disruption to Townhead's road users was a familiar concept before the various bridge rebuildings commenced, as this 1920s picture shows. The activity here could best be described as surfacing, rather than resurfacing, because the gang is laying the first modern tarmac road, replacing the previous one which was made up of compacted dirt and stones. The view looks towards the Cowgate with the old canal bridge in the background and the Boar's Head building on the right. It appears to have fallen on less happy times compared to the picture on the facing page; indeed it seems to exemplify all those decrepit and derelict things that temperance campaigners liked to associate with the 'demon drink'. In the early 1920s those campaigners took on the licensed trade in a battle that split the town and led to a deed poll, the result of which was a ban that came into effect on 27 May 1921. The looming presence of St Mary's Parish Church seems somehow to encapsulate the power that the pubs faced. The Boar's Head became a newsagents, but that failed to save the building which was demolished and replaced in 1934 by the police station. Nearly 70 years later, the police moved out to new premises and the building was converted into – a pub. Truly it seems that what goes around really does come around!

Cowgate is seen here looking south towards Townhead. On the left is the Watson Fountain, presented to the town in 1893 by Sir John Watson Bt. of Earnock, one of Scotland's biggest mine owners, who was born and brought up in Kirkintilloch, although he lived near Hamilton for most of his life. His father, also John Watson, was a stonemason from Cupar in Fife who settled in Kirkintilloch in 1814. He became a coal merchant in 1831, selling supplies brought along the Monkland & Kirkintilloch Railway, but later buying his own mine near Banknock. As business expanded he moved to the Hamilton area with his family. There young John went into business on his own, eventually owning some of the most modern and productive collieries in Scotland. They earned him enough to splash out on a fountain for his native town. The shops set back from the kerb on the left behind it were caught up in a controversy in 1904 when the town council relaid the extra wide pavement in front – and charged the full cost to the traders. Ebenezer Macindoe, who ran a painting and decorating business from the small shop partly hidden by the fountain, refused to pay. Some of his household effects and stock were seized and put up for sale, but sympathisers stepped in and bought two chairs for the whole amount. Ebenezer got his furniture back and the council got its money – but lost its credibility.

Along with Townhead, Cowgate formed the main commercial artery of the old town, and although off-street and out-of-town shopping malls have taken the buzz away from the streets today, they can still muster a bustle of shoppers to match the number of people in this view looking north along Cowgate. The Watson fountain is to the right of centre, partly obscured by a parked car. The building behind it was formerly the location of the subscription school where John Watson received his early education. Alexanders Stores, the business that took over the premises, was perhaps the most famous in Kirkintilloch's retailing history. Established in 1835, it grew to become the largest chain of hardware stores in Scotland, with branches at Ayr, Bo'ness, Falkirk, Kilsyth and even Glasgow – a nice reversal of the usual trend of city shops having country branches. The buildings in the centre background stand on High Street where it crosses the northern end of Cowgate. They have now been replaced by the impressive modern library building which superseded the original library at Camphill House.

Alexandra Street is seen here looking west. St David's Free Church, on the left, was built in the wake of a schism which rocked the Church of Scotland in 1843. The event, known as the 'Disruption', was caused by a rebellion against patronage: the right of a powerful figure to be able to appoint a minister against the wishes of the congregation. The original St David's Church in Ledgate was less than ten years old when most of the congregation left for the Free Church, which is perhaps best known for the personality of its minister from 1878 to 1892, the Revd William Patrick. During his ministry the congregation grew in numbers, but his involvement in local politics made him a controversial figure – he was chairman of the Kirkintilloch Educational Trust and founder of the temperance movement that was to have such an impact on the town. The library is named after him although it was his brother, David, a solicitor and town clerk, who gifted Camphill House to the burgh to be used as a library named after William. A new church was built in the 1920s alongside the one in this picture and is now known by the combined name of St David's Memorial Park.

This early twentieth century view looks along Northbank Road towards its junction with Park Avenue, which lies just beyond the two women ambling down the middle of the street. It would have been logical if Northbank Road, like Southbank Road, had run alongside the canal, but perversely it led away from it and it is Alexandra Street that follows the line of the waterway. Like the latter, Northbank Road was a private road until 1909 when the town council agreed with a recommendation of the Roads Committee that it should be taken over. Prior to that, in 1905, while work was being carried out on the road, funds were found to have the men on site also improve the right of way running alongside Northbank House from the north end of the road to the canal. This entailed cleaning, levelling, laying whinstone chips and repairing the badly worn steps at the canalside. The path is now sandwiched between Northbank House and the newer houses in Northbank Avenue where former provost William Fletcher lived. He was a keen photographer who captured many aspects of the town on film. One of his pictures, taken from his house, appears on page 14 and another is reproduced on page 16.

Kerr Street on a dismal day looking back towards Cowgate from where the back of Tesco's store is now. Weaving shops were developed at the street's eastern end in the early nineteenth century and one, belonging to local manufacturer James Calder, kept going until c.1910 making it the last loomshop in town. There was a toll-house at the corner of Kerr Street and Cowgate which controlled a toll bar across the main road. Kerr Street also has a tradition for learning, being the location of one of Kirkintilloch's pre-Education Act schools and subsequently Lairdsland Primary. Opposite this was the Park Church, opened in 1855 to serve a United Presbyterian congregation that broke away from the original secession church of 1735. The congregation now worships at St David's Memorial Park in Alexandra Street and the Kerr Street building is used as the Park Centre. As if to prove the Wesleyan saying that 'cleanliness is next to godliness', one Charles Goodwin opened a public baths at 13 Kerr Street in 1901, where the post office now is. He claimed to have spared no expense in equipping the facility with the latest sanitary fittings, and charged sixpence a bath. Thursday was ladies' only, but otherwise the baths were open between 9 a.m. and 9 p.m. Monday to Saturday, and for two hours before church on a Sunday morning.

Kirkintilloch's civic pride must have suffered a rude shock when the good folk of Lenzie managed to raise the cash to build a public hall there in 1892. The older town had no such facility and people had to hold meetings in a variety of places including public houses or the Temperance Hall in Alexandra Street, but a bequest from the late Provost Mackay jolted the town council into action. The legacy had to be matched with additional funds and so the council set about raising the money and finding a site. They selected one in Union Street, which was not greeted with universal approval but accepted as suitable. Construction began in 1905, and in May Provost Andrew Graham-Service conducted the ceremony to lay a memorial stone, seen here. It was a great civic occasion which also included the handing over of the fountain and

bandstand in Peel Park. When finished, the main hall and galleries could accommodate 1,200 seated people and the stage was fitted-out for theatrical performances. Keeping bang up-to-date with the times, it also had a cinematograph screen. There was some wonder expressed at the way the 12-foot wide galleries around the hall had been built with no supporting columns, and also some concern at the cost of a project which was still unfinished at the time of opening and had almost doubled in price. On 1 September 1906, three days before the official opening, the Horticultural Society held its annual exhibition there. Since then talks, dances and pantomimes have all taken place, including some political meetings where giants like Keir Hardie, George Lansbury and Ramsay MacDonald have graced the proceedings. The lesser hall was added in 1959.

Opposite: Co-operative societies grew out of the need for poorly paid and often exploited industrial workers to find a way of obtaining good, wholesome food at prices they could afford. The Kirkintilloch Equitable Co-operative Society's first shop was in the Cowgate and was followed by this branch at the corner of Broadcroft and Rochdale Place. Rochdale is regarded as the birthplace of the co-operative movement, although Scotland has a proud history in this field, with a number of small friendly and victualling societies predating 1832 when the Rochdale Friendly Co-operative Society was formed. Many more societies based on the co-operative principle were set up in Scotland following the Friendly Societies Act of 1834, with a peak of new registrations being reached in the early 1860s. By 1868 there were so many retail societies that it was possible to set up the Scottish Co-operative Wholesale Society (SCWS) to supply the shops. Kirkintilloch Equitable Co-operative Society was a late arrival on the scene, being established in 1882. This Broadcroft branch had been opened by 1887 and was followed by the large building at Townhead Bridge in 1897 plus the bakery, dairy and many other retail outlets. Branches were also established at Auchinloch, Eastside and Lenzie. The need for people to club together in the old co-operative way has diminished in recent years, but the movement has left its mark in the confident inscriptions carved on the face of some surviving buildings.

Canal Street runs between Eastside and the canal on the east side of the Luggie Water. The town's first gasworks was set up at the south (canal) end of the street in 1838 by a private concern called the Kirkintilloch Gas Light Company. While it supplied the gas, the civic authority, the police commissioners, were responsible for providing the street lighting facilities, but it was not a cosy situation. The commissioners wanted to control the gas supply and, taking advantage of the Burghs Gas Supply Act of 1876, bought the gasworks from the company. They soon discovered that the restricted site would make expansion impossible and replaced the works with a new one at Back o' Loch in 1908. Another industrial concern established in Canal Street was the soaperie of the Caurnie Chemical Company whose soaps made ' "whites" white and "colours" bright'. Industrial sites in Canal Street were also made available to businesses attracted to the town in the 1960s by the Glasgow overspill scheme. The street's other claim to fame was being the site of the town's railway station, which was established at its north end.

In the early years of railway development, Kirkintilloch must have been one of the best-served towns in Scotland. From the 1820s, passengers could travel along the Monkland & Kirkintilloch (M&K) line to Coatbridge and from there take another train to Glasgow. In 1842, when the main Edinburgh & Glasgow Railway was opened, Kirky folk could walk the mile or two to Lenzie and take a train directly from there to either city and all points in between. The two railways therefore placed Kirkintilloch within striking distance of the country's main centres before some communities had seen a puff of locomotive smoke, and it got better. In 1848 the Campsie Branch Railway was laid from the main line through Kirkintilloch where the new station was built at the end of Canal Street. The tracks carried on over Eastside to Lennoxtown, and were later extended to Aberfoyle. After the Second World War, however, the vulnerability of Kirkintilloch's early railway advantages began to become apparent: the town was served by branch lines, and as road transport increased these were susceptible to economic and political pressures. Passenger services on the Campsie Branch were progressively cut back until 1964 when those between Kirkintilloch and Lenzie ran for the last time. The station is seen here in June 1961 just before its closure.

The railways and canal provided Kirkintilloch with one of the best transport services of any inland town in Scotland. This made it hugely attractive to industry, and the iron industry in particular. Iron-working had begun on an industrial scale in Scotland with the setting up of the Carron Ironworks in 1760. The next significant development was the hot blast process of smelting developed by James Beaumont Neilson in 1828. A massive expansion of blast furnace activity followed, particularly at Coatbridge, but Carron also adapted to the new method. Scotland was now producing vast quantities of cheap pig-iron and numerous foundries and forges were set up to turn it into a bewildering range of products. With Coatbridge and Glasgow on one side and Falkirk on the other, Kirkintilloch became part of an industry that made 50% of Britain's cast iron products. The town's first foundry was set up about 1836 south of the canal and west of the Luggie. The opposite side of the canal was claimed in 1880 when the Lion Foundry was established. It specialised in decorative castings – gates, railings, bandstands, fountains etc. – but in the 1930s started making telephone boxes, a product that kept it in business until 1984.

Heavy industries didn't come much heavier than the iron industry. The basic raw materials – pig-iron and coal or coke – were very heavy, and because they came from a limited range of suppliers the canal provided the ideal way to bring them into the foundries. The finished products were also heavy, but they had to go to a wider variety of customers and usually left by rail. The conjunction of the Monkland & Kirkintilloch Railway with the canal attracted another foundry, the Star. It was set up in 1861 by one Alexander Smith, and in 1867 was taken over by the firm of Cameron & Roberton. They gave it a new name, the South Bank Ironworks, but Kirkintilloch folk seemed to have a liking for old names and continued to call it the Star up to its closure in 1981. Here foundrymen are proudly posing with some drainpipes. Whilst these may seem rather prosaic, in those days people took pride in making such items and they made them well. The foundry specialised in rainwater pipes, gutters and other such items of architectural ironwork.

Before any iron could be cast in a foundry a mould had to be made for it, and that's where these men, the pattern makers, came in. They had to translate a drawing or model into a perfect example of the intended iron product, but made in wood. It was an immensely skilled job practised by very fine craftsmen, and some of their work can be seen here in the workshops at the South Bank Ironworks. In the foreground is a conductor pipe head with the date 1911 clearly visible on it: this must also be a good indication of when the picture was taken. Using patterns made in this workshop, the moulders, working in vast smoke-filled sheds, pressed the wooden forms into a special kind of sand contained in box-like frames. They left a channel for the molten iron to be poured into, and when this had cooled the sand was removed to reveal the finished article. Inevitably the molten iron shrank as it cooled and so the pattern-makers and moulders had to allow for this, particularly when making a complex item, like a bandstand, when numerous different casts had to fit together.

In the late nineteenth and early twentieth centuries there were three collieries of moderate size on the eastern side of Kirkintilloch. Auchenreoch was to the north beside the Kilsyth Road, Woodilee was to the south-east and between them was Meiklehill, a pit of uncertain age and with extensive underground workings. It was located close to the modern-day district of Rosebank and was linked by railway to the canal where a couper could tip wagons of coal directly into boats. This little pug engine, built in 1886 by Dübs of Queen's Park, Glasgow, moved Meiklehill's coal

wagons around. The pit worked seams of steam and coking coal, and its coke ovens were a magnet at night-time for homeless men who used to sleep beside them for warmth. The colliery was being operated by James Gardner & Sons in the 1890s when it was taken over by James Wood Ltd., who in turn was absorbed into a large grouping of small coal companies known as United Collieries about 1902. Meiklehill came under local management again when the Woodilee Coal & Coke Company bought it in 1908, and it continued in production until the 1920s. Despite closure the pit continued to have an effect on the area because its waste bing started to burn, spreading sulphurous fumes across the neighbourhood until it was levelled in 1964.

With canals and railways playing a major part in Kirkintilloch's industrial and transport history, it is perhaps not surprising that it had an industry associated with motor transport too. The bodywork of this little van was built at the Eastside works of James Martin. He was the son of a Tintock weaver who worked on the canal and at an ironstone mine before setting up on Eastside as a cartwright. Moving with the times, he turned from this horse-hauled form of transport to newfangled motor vehicles when they started to appear. Setting himself up as a coachbuilder in Kilsyth Road, he produced a wide variety of vehicle body types, mainly on chassis supplied by Ford or Fordson. The firm continued after his death, opening a car showroom and service station in Cowgate in 1930. Another local coachbuilder was John McLay who started in business with a cycle shop and moved into building vehicle bodies on Morris chassis. The McLay name is still to be seen as a car and van rental business in East High Street.

Kirkintilloch's handloom weavers commonly wove linen cloth for manufacturers based in large towns like Glasgow. These entrepreneurs sold the cloth on to other customers and by charging them more and paying the weavers less could make a tidy sum. Things started to change for the weavers early in the nineteenth century when cotton replaced linen as the main cloth, and large textile mills took over from the handlooms. Initially, as at New Lanark, these mills were water-powered, but with the application of steam power they could be set up anywhere. The longest-lasting mill in Kirkintilloch was that of James Slimon & Co. which was built in Milton Road in 1867. The mill survived a fire early in its life, and with up to 300 looms on the premises and over 200 employees – mainly women and girls – it continued in production making cotton fabrics suitable for shirts, skirts and fashionable garments. It closed briefly in 1929, but didn't finally shut up shop until the following year.

Slimon's redundant mill building was bought by one of Scotland's premier electrical engineering companies, Mavor & Coulson Ltd. They called it the Kelvinside Works and set up a subsidiary operation there under the name of M. & C. Switchgear Ltd. The windows and other features suggest that this M. & C. office has been set up in the same room as the mill on the facing page. Mavor & Coulson started operations as electrical engineers in the east end of Glasgow in 1883, but soon began to specialise in mining equipment and helped the industry to move from pick, shovel and pony to machine cutting, loading and conveying. M. & C.'s move to Kirkintilloch came at a time when British mining was struggling, but the company kept busy, exporting its machines all over the world. It prospered following the nationalisation of the British coal industry in 1947 when old pits were upgraded and a massive investment was made in new capacity. As the coal industry began to cut back, the company amalgamated with its closest rival, Anderson–Boyes of Motherwell, to become Anderson–Mavor, and later, Anderson Strathclyde PLC. This in turn was taken over by an American company, Long–Airdox, which closed the Scottish machine-mining industry down in 1997.

When Glasgow cotton spinner John Bartholomew died, his Broomhill House and its accompanying farm were bought by the Association for the Relief of Incurables in Glasgow and the West of Scotland. This charitable body aimed to provide a home for people suffering from cancer, tuberculosis and other incurable conditions. The first patients were admitted in 1876 and over time the original house was extended and adapted to accommodate over 100 patients and staff. This picture shows female patients in their day room where they could spend time knitting and sewing items which were offered at annual sales of work to raise money for the charity. Residents or their families also had to pay for accommodation to ensure that the charity

remained solvent, such was the precarious nature of funding for patients like these before the NHS was set up. There was high drama in 1904 when a fire broke out in the ceiling space of one of the wards. It was discovered by a nurse who alerted the matron, Miss Whitecross, who raised the alarm. One of the patients, George Gordon, had the task of ringing the alarm bell which he did with such gusto it was heard on the other side of Antermony Loch. The home had made good provision for fire-fighting and so staff were able to contain the blaze until the fire brigade arrived to put it out. If fire wasn't enough of a problem at a home catering for the infirm, the building's location beside the Kelvin meant that it was often cut off by floods.

One of the prime movers in setting up Broomhill Home was local philanthropist Miss Beatrice Clugston, but this remarkable lady was not content to stop there. She persuaded a friend, Miss Martha Brown of Lanfine in Ayrshire, to bequeath money to the associations for incurables in both the Glasgow and Edinburgh areas to set up homes for terminally ill sufferers of phthisis – pulmonary tuberculosis. The Glasgow association built Lanfine Home adjacent to Broomhill and it was opened in May 1904 by the Duchess of Montrose, another lady who devoted much of her time and money to this unglamorous area of healthcare. Broomhill Home's sale of work was held on the same day and benefited from having so many invited guests to sell produce to. Lanfine Home was not a sanatorium – its patients were too ill to recover – but provided a comfortable place for them to be nursed to the end of their lives. The original L-shaped brick and roughcast building, with red sandstone facings and red tiled roof, could cater for eighteen patients, but this number was increased over time as the building was extended. Glass-roofed verandas, one of which is seen here, allowed bedridden patients to enjoy fresh air and sunshine, while the building was sited to shield them from the cold east wind. Both Broomhill and Lanfine were absorbed into the NHS when it was set up in 1948. Lanfine was used for geriatric patients while Broomhill continued to care for the chronically sick until both establishments were closed in 1995.

Kirkintilloch's first major council housing scheme at Back o' Loch was inaugurated in May 1921 by Provost Thomas Gibson and Bailie John Shanks, convenor of the Housing Committee. They each laid a commemorative stone at different sections of the scheme. These houses in Loch Road were part of the development of 100 four-apartment and 100 three-apartment homes, of which 64 were built as four in a block, two-up and two-down. As well as living room and bedrooms, each new home had a bathroom, scullery, larder and coal cellar, hot and cold water, gas copper for washing clothes and gardens front and back. The total cost of the scheme was £194,500, which at today's values might just buy one four-apartment house. The houses were a huge improvement on the run-down older property they replaced, a point alluded to by the provost in his address. Referring to the existing damp, insanitary houses he suggested that because the new homes were built on high ground, with good dry foundations, they would be dry houses in a dry town, a reference to the impending prohibition of licensed premises. Completion of the scheme sparked a scramble by public transport operators to attract the new residents. Rival bus companies offered services from Loch Road and the railway weighed in with a new station called Back o' Loch Halt (inset).

Kirkintilloch Town Council's extensive programme of housebuilding was to some extent dictated by the alarming level of squalor that the town's old streets had sunk to. The degree of deterioration was highlighted by the burgh surveyor in 1914. Out of 1,852 houses he found that only 878 were habitable as they stood, 802 were in need of repair and 172 were uninhabitable, a figure that would have been higher had modern standards been applied. 361 of the houses were only single apartments. The council's desire to do something about the problem had to be put on hold during the First World War, but when that was over things started to move. The Back o' Loch houses were the first of a concerted push through the 1920s and 30s which saw over 1,200 houses completed by the Second World War, including these in Redbrae Road. The pace continued after the war with the 1920s/30s figure being doubled by 1960 and more houses continuing to be built. Many of these were part of the Glasgow overspill scheme which was designed to ease the city's housing problem by providing homes in outlying places. Industries were also given financial incentives to relocate.

Nestling beside the Luggie Water, Waterside remained in rural isolation until Kirkintilloch's housing programme stretched the built-up area east past Oxgang. Today the river is seen as enhancing the village, but in times past it was regarded as a source of power and the means of earning a living. There were two mills in the vicinity: Duntiblae was originally a meal mill which was later used for making spades, while higher up the river Waterside Mill was also used as a forge. It was built in 1779 and originally involved in the linen trade which flourished in the village, its function being to remove the skin from flax stalks. Prior to this operation the stalks had to be soaked in water to soften the hard outer layer so that it could be removed more easily. The latter process could be achieved by hand using a scutcher's handle, but the mill did it faster with a 'Flemish Wheel', a device like a series of rotating scutcher's handles which produced a greater quantity of raw linen than the hand process. The mills were not large employers and many more Watersiders worked with the product of the mill as weavers. Their well-being was catered for by two other industrial enterprises in the village, a distillery and a gasworks, which is seen here in ruins on the right. Its demise was hastened by the company chairman who refused to give the only employee, the man who made the gas, a pay rise. He decided to run the works himself, but had no experience and managed to wreck three retorts and lose large amounts of gas by failing to repair leaks in the pipes.

Waterside was close to a number of small coal workings and was within half a mile of Wester Gartshore Colliery. These houses, the Wester Gartshore Rows, were erected for the miners working at the pit, which was sunk by the Wallace family of Solsgirth in the late nineteenth century to work seams of anthracitic, coking and steam coals. The Cadzow Coal Company took it over in 1914, erected pithead baths in 1939 and was still operating the colliery at the time of nationalisation in 1947. Production ceased in 1950, but despite closure the pithead buildings remained in use as the offices of the National Coal Board's Kilsyth Sub-Area, with the baths becoming the planning office. Some of the buildings remain, but the most obvious reminder of the old pit is its distinctive peaked waste bing beside the main Edinburgh to Glasgow railway line. It has survived for over half a century because careful picking and fine screens at the colliery meant that very little coal was deposited on it, so unlike Meiklehill's bing it never spontaneously combusted. Also, none of the companies that recover coal from old bings have yet deemed it worth their while to work on. Wester Gartshore's closure marked the end of deep mining in and around Waterside and Kirkintilloch.

In the days when local football clubs could command great popular support, Kirkintilloch had a number of teams. These included Kirkintilloch United, Kirkintilloch Harp and Hillhead Rovers, a team that enjoyed some success in county cup and league competitions. One club, however, outstripped them all – Kirkintilloch Rob Roy – the Rabs. It was formed in 1878 and, after playing at a number of grounds, eventually settled in 1926 at Adamslie Park, the old home ground of Kirkintilloch Harp. The club has played most of its football in junior leagues, latterly being part of the Central Region of the Scottish Junior FA. It won the Central League Championship in season 1961–2, a year that also brought success in the Coronation and Dunbartonshire Cups and the Scottish Junior Cup – a four-trophy haul unmatched before or since. The Rabs had previously won the Scottish Junior Cup in 1921 and 1943, but such success has been difficult to achieve lately. This picture shows the team in 1892 with those famous red and black stripes running vertically, as distinct from the hooped shirts of later years.